A Parent's Guic Education for 8-12 Year Olds

How to talk and educate your child about sex, relationship and puberty

By

KATHY W. LISA

Kathy W. Lisa

TABLE OF CONTENTS

INTRODUCTION

It is never too early to start sex education. A parent can be the most sex-positive and affirming influence on a child, this is because sex should be approached as a natural and positive part of life.

Sex education should not be viewed as a single event, but rather as an ongoing conversation between parent and child.

Parents who want to begin sex education with their children have a wealth of options at their disposal.

The most important thing is to approach the topic with openness, honesty, and respect.

It is also important to remember that sex education is an ongoing process and that children will have new questions and concerns at different stages of their development.

Here are some suggestions if you don't know where to begin:

- Speak in a matter-of-fact manner about sex.

-Use the correct terminology for body components and actions.

- Be accessible to your child's inquiries.

- Respect your child's privacy.

- Encourage your child to ask questions.

- Seek out additional resources if needed.

Sex education is a vital part of parenting, and it is never too early to start.

By approaching sex in a positive and open way, parents can help their children develop a healthy attitude towards sex and relationships.

Sex education should not be viewed as a single event, but rather as an ongoing conversation between parent and child.

Most importantly, remember to approach the topic with openness, honesty, and respect.

This book will serve as a guide for parents who want to sex education with their 8-12-year-olds.

It will cover topics such as why sex education is important, how to approach the topic with your child, what resources are available, and how to answer common questions.

By the end of this book, you will have the tools you need to start sex education with your child in a positive and affirming way.

CHAPTER ONE

The Importance of Sex Education

Sex education is an incredibly important and often overlooked aspect of parenting.

It is crucial for both parents and children to have a basic understanding of sex-related topics so that they can communicate openly about these issues as they arise.

This communication can help kids feel more comfortable talking about their bodies, asking questions, and making safer choices when it comes to sexual health. There are a number of reasons why sex education is so important for children.

For one thing, research shows that teens who receive comprehensive sex education are less likely to engage in risky behavior like having unprotected sex or using drugs or alcohol before having sex.

They also tend to delay the onset of sexual activity until later on in life, compared to those who only learn abstinence-only education.

Another key benefit of sex education is that it can help kids develop healthy relationships and learn about consent, communication, and respect for themselves and others.

Additionally, this education can equip children with the tools they need to make informed decisions about their sexual health, such as how to practice safer sex or how to get tested for STIs/STDs.

So if you're a parent looking to start having more open and honest conversations with your kids about sex, there are a number of strategies that you can try.

First, it's important to choose the right time and place for these discussions - ideally somewhere where you won't be interrupted or distracted.

Then, try approaching the conversation from a non-judgmental perspective, and be sure to listen to your child's concerns and questions. The key is to empower your children with the knowledge they need to make safe and healthy choices throughout their lives.

1. Begin by discussing the need for sex education, exploring why it is essential to equip your child with the knowledge and tools they need to make safe, healthy decisions about their bodies and relationships.

2. Next, examine some of the specific topics that should be included in a comprehensive sex education curriculum (do this by taking a look at what they are being thought in school) such as consent, sexual health and safety, STIs and pregnancy prevention, etc.

3. Consider the challenges that exist in providing effective sex education programs, such as cultural and religious norms, lack of resources.

4. Finally, discuss how these challenges can be overcome through collaboration between you and your child. Make them understand why you are the only person they should trust when it comes to sex education and everything concerning them. BUILD TRUST!

Overall, the importance of sex education cannot be overstated. By ensuring that young people are equipped with the knowledge and tools they need to make informed decisions about their bodies and relationships, we can help them lead safer, healthier lives and set them up for success in all areas of life.

Emotional and Physical Aspects of sex in 8-12-year-olds

There are many emotional and physical aspects of sex that can be confusing for 8-12-year-olds. This book will help to explain some of the basics so that you can make more informed decisions about your child's sexual activity.

The physical aspects of sex include everything from how our bodies work during sex, to how we can protect ourselves from STDs and pregnancy. It is important to understand these things so that you can make healthy choices and lessons for your child.

The emotional aspects of sex can be just as confusing. You need to make sure that your teen understands that sex can be a great experience if they are ready for it and there is time and age for everything.

But it is important to make sure that you are ready emotionally and physically before you take the plunge.

3 conversation starters for parents when teaching their children about sex

When did you first learn about sex?

You can begin by sharing your own experience with sex education, and how it made you feel. This will help set the tone for an open and honest conversation.

What do you think about sex?

It's important to get an idea of your child's thoughts and feelings on sex before starting a conversation. This will help you gauge their level of comfort and understanding.

Where do you think you would go for more information?

Encourage your child to come to you with any questions or concerns they have about sex.

Let them know that you are always available to talk, and provide resources for further information.

It is important to note that sex education is an ongoing conversation, not a one-time talk. As your child grows and develops, they will have new questions and concerns.

Be sure to keep the lines of communication open, so they feel comfortable coming to you with anything they need to know.

CHAPTER TWO

Beginning the Conversation

It can be difficult to know how to start sex education with your child. You may be wondering when the right time is, what topics to cover, and how to approach the conversation.

Here are some pointers to get you going:

1.**Start young** - It's never too early to start talking to your youngster about sex and relationships.

By starting early, you can make sure they have accurate information and feel comfortable coming to you with questions or concerns.

2. **Be age-appropriate** - Make sure the information you're sharing is appropriate for your child's age and development level. There's no need to go into explicit detail if they're not ready for it.

3. **Be open and honest** - Answer your child's questions as honestly as you can. If you don't know the answer to something, look it up together or find someone who can help.

4. **Be supportive** - Let your child know that you're there for them no matter what. They may make mistakes, but you'll always love and support them.

Start early and be open and honest with your child. By doing so, you can ensure they have accurate information and feel comfortable coming to you with any questions or concerns.

Sex Education for 12+ Kids

As your teenager enters adolescence, they will likely become more curious about sex and their own bodies.

It's important to provide them with accurate information about sex so that they can make informed decisions when the time comes.

There are a few key things you should cover in sex education for 12+ kids:

- The physical changes of puberty, including the development of sexual organs and secondary sex characteristics.

- The reproductive system and how it works. This includes information on periods, ovulation, fertilization, and contraception.

- The emotional and social aspects of sex, such as peer pressure, consent and communication.

- The risks associated with sex, including sexually transmitted diseases and unplanned pregnancy.

However, sex education is not just about the facts. It's also about helping your teenager to develop a positive attitude towards sex and their own sexuality. This includes teaching them about pleasure, respect, and communication.

Kids in the 21st century are growing up in a world where sex is everywhere - on TV, in movies, and on the internet. It's important that they have accurate information so that they can make informed decisions about sex.

As a parent, you are the best person to provide sex education for your teenager.

If you're not sure where to start, there are plenty of resources available to help you plan sex education for 12+ kids.

The most important thing is to be open and honest with your teenager about sex. This will help them to feel comfortable talking about sex with you, and it will also ensure that they receive accurate information.

Sex Education: what works and what doesn't

It's no secret that sex education is a controversial topic. Just think about all the debates surrounding what should be taught in schools.

Some people believe that sex education should be abstinence-only, while others think it should be more comprehensive, teaching about both abstinence and contraception.

There's no easy answer when it comes to sex education. But one thing is for sure: parents play a vital role in educating their children about sex.

No matter what your personal beliefs are, it's important to have an open and honest conversation with your teenager about sex.

Here are some things to keep in mind as you talk to your teenager about sex:

- Be open and honest: It's important to be open and honest with your teenager about sex. This means being willing to answer any questions they have, no matter how awkward it may feel.

- Be respectful: It's also important to be respectful of your teenager's feelings and beliefs. Remember, you're not trying to convince them of anything, you're just trying to provide information and answer their questions.

- Keep it simple: When it comes to sex education, less is more. Try to focus on the basics, like human anatomy, reproduction, and sexually transmitted infections (STIs). There's no need to get into the nitty-gritty details unless your teenager asks for them.

- Be prepared: If you're not comfortable talking about sex, that's OK. Just be sure to do some research ahead of time so you're prepared to answer your teenager's questions.

Helping Your Child Understand Different Ways People Show Affection

Sex education can be a bit tricky. There are different ways that people show affection and not all of them involve sex.

It is important to teach your teenager about the different ways people show affection so they can better understand their own emotions and the emotions of others.

Here are some different ways people show affection:

1. Physical touch - This includes things like hugging, kissing, and holding hands.

Everything about Consent that Your Child Must Know

When it comes to teaching consent in sex education for 8-12 year olds, it is important to focus on the concept of consent, not on the details of sex.

This means talking about respecting others' boundaries and feelings and understanding that everyone has the right to say yes or no when it comes to physical contact.

It is also important to discuss consent openly with your child and make sure they understand that consent needs to be present at all times - even between two people who know each other.

Help your child understand that consent can be changed or withdrawn at any time, and must be respected by all parties involved.

To help explain consent in an age appropriate way, you can use everyday examples such as making a snack together, playing a game, or using the family computer.

Explain to your child that consent needs to be obtained before each activity and can be withdrawn at any time - even if it was given earlier on.

Let's say your child wants to play a game of tag with a friend. Before they start the game, it is essential for them to communicate consent.

Even though it is just a game, they need to ensure their friend is comfortable with the rules and wants to play.

You might ask them, "Are you okay with playing tag?

Is it okay if I chase you? Are there any rules we should follow?"

This will help your child understand consent before engaging in physical activities.

Another way to explain consent is through stories. Tell your children a story about two friends playing in the park.

For example, Friend A wants to jump on the trampoline but Friend B doesn't want to join in. In this case, Friend A must respect Friend B's wishes and find another activity they both agree upon.

This shows how important it is for all parties involved to communicate their feelings and opinions, and respect each other's decisions.

2. Words of affirmation - This can be things like saying "I love you," "I'm proud of you," or simply expressing gratitude.

3. Quality time - This involves giving someone your undivided attention, whether it's talking, going on a date, or just spending time together.

4. Acts of service - This can be things like cooking, cleaning, or running errands for someone.

5. Gifts - This is a way of showing someone you care about them by giving them something thoughtful.

It's important to remember that not everyone expresses affection in the same way. Some people may prefer one type of affection over another. It's also important to remember that just because someone doesn't express affection in a physical way, it doesn't mean they don't care about you.

If you're not sure how someone is feeling, the best thing to do is ask them directly. This can be a scary conversation to have, but it's worth it to avoid misunderstandings.

CHAPTER THREE

How to Use Scenarios for Sex Education

When sex education is taught in schools, the focus is often on the physical aspects of sex and reproduction.

However, it is also important to talk about the emotional aspects of sex, and how to have healthy and respectful relationships.

Scenarios can be a helpful way to start these discussions, by getting kids thinking about different situations they might encounter and how they would deal with them.

Here are some examples of scenarios that could be used in sex education:

- You are at a party with your friends and someone offers you a drink. You know that you shouldn't drink alcohol because you're under age, but everyone else is doing it. What do you do?

- You are in a relationship and things are starting to get physical. You want to have sex, but your partner doesn't seem ready. What do you do?

- You are out on a date with someone you really like. They try to pressure you into having sex even though you've said you're not ready. What do you do?

Talking through these kinds of scenarios can help your kids to think about what they would do in different situations, and to start to develop their own values and boundaries.

It can also be a valuable opportunity for parents to share their own views on sex and relationships, and to offer guidance and support.

Scenarios are important in sex education because:

- They help kids to think about different situations they might encounter.

- They help to develop values and boundaries.

- They offer an opportunity for parents to share their own views on sex and relationships.

As a parent, you can use scenarios to start discussions with your teenager about sex and relationships.

You can also encourage them to think about different situations they might encounter, and how they would deal with them.

If you are a teacher, you can use scenarios in the classroom to get students thinking about different situations they might encounter, and how to deal with them.

If you are a youth worker, you can use scenarios with the young people you work with to get them thinking about different situations they might encounter, and how to deal with them.

Some possible discussion questions that could be used alongside the above scenarios are:

- What do you think the right thing to do is in this situation?

- What do you think the consequences of each option could be?

- What values and boundaries do you think are important in a relationship?

- What do you think the consequences of not respecting someone's values and boundaries could be?

- How can you communicate your own values and boundaries to a partner?

These discussion questions can help to get kids thinking about the different options available to them in each situation, and the possible consequences of each option.

They can also help to develop their own values and boundaries, and to understand the importance of communicating these to a partner.

Sex education for is important because it helps them develop their own values and boundaries. Scenarios are one way sex education can achieve this goal.

When sex education is taught in schools, the focus is often on the physical aspects of sex and reproduction.

However, it is also important to talk about the emotional aspects of sex, and how to have healthy and respectful relationships.

Here are some examples of scenarios that could be used in sex education:

- You are at a party with your friends and someone offers you a drink. You know that you shouldn't drink alcohol because you're under age, but everyone else is doing it. What do you do?

- You are in a relationship and things are starting to get physical. You want to have sex, but your partner doesn't seem ready. What do you do?

- You are out on a date with someone you really like. They try to pressure you into having sex even though you've said you're not ready. What do you do?

Talking through these kinds of scenarios can help kids to think about what they would do in different situations, and to start to develop their own values and boundaries.

It can also be a valuable opportunity for parents to share their own views on sex and relationships, and to offer guidance and support.

Scenarios are important in sex education because:

- They help kids to think about different situations they might encounter.

- They help to develop values and boundaries.

- They offer an opportunity for parents to share their own views on sex and relationships.

As a parent, you can use scenarios to start discussions with your teenager about sex and relationships.

You can also encourage them to think about different situations they might encounter, and how they would deal with them.

If you are a teacher, you can use scenarios in the classroom to get students thinking about different situations they might encounter, and how to deal with them.

If you are a youth worker, you can use scenarios with the young people you work with to get them thinking about different situations they might encounter, and how to deal with them.

Some possible discussion questions that could be used alongside the above scenarios are:

- What do you think the right thing to do in this situation?

- What do you think the consequences of each option could be?

- What values and boundaries do you think are important in a relationship?

- What do you think the consequences of not respecting someone's values and boundaries could be?

- How can you communicate your own values and boundaries to a partner?

These discussion questions can help to get kids thinking about the different options available to them in each situation, and the possible consequences of each option.

They can also help to develop their own values and boundaries and to understand the importance of communicating these to a partner.

Natural Progression of Affection in Relationships: The Answer

As your child enters the teenage years, they will likely start to express more interest in sex and relationships.

It is important to provide them with accurate information about sex and help them understand how to develop healthy relationships.

One question that parents often ask is whether there is a natural progression of affection in a relationship. The answer is that there is no one right way for every relationship to progress.

Some couples may move quickly from holding hands to kissing, while others may take things slower.

What is important is that both partners feel comfortable with the pace of the relationship and are able to communicate their needs and boundaries.

If you are concerned about your teenager's sex education or relationships, talk to their doctor or a counsellor. They can provide you with more information and resources.

Sex education can most certainly help when it comes to the natural progression of affection in relationships!

It is important for kids to learn about sex and relationships so they can develop healthy ones.

Without sex education, some teens may think that there is only one way for a relationship to progress (quickly from holding hands to kissing, for example).

This could lead to pressure on one or both partners, and ultimately discomfort.

With sex education, however, teens will know that there is no one right way for a relationship to progress.

They will feel more comfortable communicating their needs and boundaries, which is essential for a healthy relationship.

If you are concerned about your teenager's sex education or relationships, talk to their doctor or a counselor.

Does Biology or Social Experience Determine How People/Children Feel About Sex?

It's a question that has puzzled scientists and sex educators for years: does biology or social experience determine how people feel about sex?

A new study published in the journal Nature may have found an answer.

The study, conducted by researchers at the University of Zurich, looked at the sex lives of fruit flies.

The team found that when fruit flies were exposed to sex pheromones, they became more attracted to members of the opposite sex.

However, when the fruit flies were raised in a social environment that was lacking in sex pheromones, they showed no such preference.

This suggests that it is social experience, rather than biology, that determines how people feel about sex.

The findings could have implications for sex education, as they suggest that teaching children about sex and relationships from an early age could help them to develop healthy attitudes towards sex.

So what does this mean for parents and teachers? It's important to remember that every child is different, and there is no one-size-fits-all approach to sex education.

However, the findings of this study suggest that it's important to start talking about sex and relationships with children from an early age, in order to help them develop healthy attitudes towards sex.

Sex is a touchy subject for many people. It can be seen as taboo, and often people feel uncomfortable talking about it openly.

So, does sex education play a role in how people feel about sex?

There are two main schools of thought on this issue. The first belief is that sex is a natural and normal part of life, and that sex education should be taught in a way that is open and honest.

The second belief is that sex is something that should be private, and that sex education should be limited to the basics.

So, which viewpoint is correct? Unfortunately, there is no easy answer. Both biology and social experience play a role in how people feel about sex.

On the one hand, sex is a natural biological function. It is a part of human nature, and it is something that we are wired to do.

Sex education should reflect this, and should be taught in a way that is open and honest.

On the other hand, sex is also a social construct. It is something that we learn about through our culture, our families, and our peers.

Sex education should take this into account, and should be limited to the basics.

Ultimately, it is up to each individual to decide how they feel about sex. Sex education can play a role in this, but it is not the only factor.

Biology and social experience both play a role in shaping our views on sex this is why it is important to consider both when making decisions about sex education.

So, as a teacher or parent, it is important to understand that both play a vital role in sexual orientation of both adults and children, begin shaping the mind of your children when they are younger, that way, they'd have no issues making the right decisions growing up.

CHAPTER FOUR

Dealing with Your Childs Sexual Orientation as a Parent

Parenting a child with a different sexual orientation can present its own unique challenges. Here are some tips for parents dealing with their child's sexual orientation:

-Talk to your child about their feelings and experiences. It is important to create an open and safe environment where your child feels comfortable talking about their sexuality.

-Educate yourself on different sexual orientations. This will help you better understand your child and how they are feeling.

-Be accepting and supportive of your child. They need your support and love now, more than anything else.

-Encourage your child to be true to themselves. They deserve to live their life authentically and should not have to hide who they are.

-Talk to other parents who have children with different sexual orientations. They can provide valuable insight and support.

Parenting is never easy, but it is important to remember that your child needs your love and support no matter what.

If you are struggling to accept your child's sexual orientation, seek out professional help. Your child deserves to be loved and accepted for who they are.

As a parent, it is normal to feel protective of your child and their future.

You want them to be happy and to have a good life, free from discrimination and harassment.

It can be difficult to accept that your child is not heterosexual, but it is important to remember that this does not change who they are as a person.

They are still the same wonderful human being that you have always loved and cared for.

There are a few important things you can do to support your child:

- Listen to them: Allow them to share their experiences and feelings with you without judgment. This will help them feel supported and loved.

- Be there for them: Let them know that you are there for them, no matter what. This will provide a sense of security during tough times.

Sexual orientation can be a sensitive topic, but it is important to create an open and safe environment for your child to express themselves. By doing so, you will help them to feel happy and loved for who they are.

Discussing Gender Identity

Parenting and gender identity can be difficult topics to navigate. As a parent, you want to do what is best for your child.

When it comes to gender identity, there are a few things to keep in mind.

First and foremost, it is important to remember that gender is not the same as sex. Sex refers to the biological characteristics of a person, while gender refers to the social and cultural expectations around how a person should behave.

Just because someone is born with certain sex characteristics does not mean they have to identify with a specific gender.

It is also important to understand that gender identity is not a choice. It is something that people feel internally and cannot change.

Accepting your child's gender identity is an important step in parenting them effectively.

The most crucial thing is to be understanding and flexible.

Parenting gender identity can be a difficult journey but it is important to remember that you are not alone.

Your child's gender identity is something that you as a parent have a lot of influence over. You can help your child to understand and express their gender in a way that is comfortable for them.

One of the most important things you can do is to provide your child with accurate information about gender.

This can help them to make informed choices about their own identity. It is also important to be supportive and accepting of your child's choices regarding their gender identity.

You can also play a role in shaping your child's gender identity by modeling positive behavior yourself. For example, if you are a man who is comfortable expressing his feminine side, this can encourage your son to do the same.

If you are a woman who is confident in her masculinity, this can inspire your daughter to express her own masculine side.

Ultimately, the goal is to raise a happy and healthy child who feels comfortable in their own skin. By providing support and love, you can help your child to reach this goal.

Handling your child's gender identity can be a difficult task, but it is one that is important to get right.

With the right approach, you can help your child to understand and express their gender in a way that is comfortable for them.

You can shape your child's gender identity by doing the following;

1. Providing accurate information about gender

2. Being supportive and accepting of your child's choices

3. Modeling positive behavior yourself

4. Creating a safe and supportive environment for your child

5. Encouraging your child to be themselves

6. Teaching your child about respect for others

7. Helping your child to understand their body and their feelings

8. Talking about puberty in an age-appropriate way

9. Allowing your child to express their gender in their own way

10. Supporting your child through any difficult times

Understanding and Managing your Childs Gender Expression

It's normal for 8-12-year-olds to start expressing themselves in new and different ways.

They might experiment with their hair, clothes, and interests. This is part of discovering who they are.

As your child begins to express their gender in new ways, you might have questions or concerns. You might wonder if your child is transgender or gender nonconforming.

Here are some things to keep in mind:

- All children explore and experiment with different aspects of their identity. It's common for children to try on different identities during this phase of development.

- There is no one right way to express gender. Each person gets to decide how they want to express their gender.

- It's OK to ask your child questions about their gender expression. You can also talk to a trusted adult, like a doctor or school counselor, if you have questions or concerns.

Encouraging your child to express their gender in the way that feels right for them is one of the best things you can do as a parent. It can help your child feel good about themselves and build self-confidence.

Gender expression is different from sex. Sex is the biological characteristics of a person, for example, the sex chromosomes a person has, their hormones, and their reproductive organs.

Gender is the way people see themselves and express themselves to the world around them.

Help and Support

Sexuality is a normal and healthy part of life. It's something that we all have, regardless of whether we're straight, gay, lesbian, bisexual or transgender.

And just like any other aspect of our lives, parenting plays a vital role in helping our children understand and feel comfortable with their sexuality.

Unfortunately, there's still a lot of stigma surrounding sex and sexuality, which can make it difficult for parents to talk to their kids about these topics.

Here is a recap;

1. parenting- while it may be difficult to talk about sexuality with your child, it is important to be open and honest in order to provide them with the support they need.

2. Sex education- While sex education is not always part of the curriculum in schools, there are a number of ways you can ensure your child receives accurate information about their sexuality.

3. Sexuality- Sexuality is a normal and healthy part of who we are. It is important for children to understand that there is no right or wrong way to express their sexuality. If your child is struggling with their sexuality.

4. Parenting- while it may be difficult to talk about sexuality with your child, it is important to be open and honest in order to provide them with the support they need.

5. Sex education- While sex education is not always part of the curriculum in schools, there are a number of ways you

can ensure your child receives accurate information about their sexuality.

It's important to teach your child about relationships early on. By understanding relationship dynamics, your child can develop healthier and more positive relationships with others.

As a parent, you are your child's first teacher when it comes to learning about relationships.

You can set a good example by maintaining healthy and positive relationships with your own partner, family, and friends.

You can also talk to your child about relationship issues, such as communication, conflict resolution, and respect.

By teaching your child about relationships, you can help them develop the skills they need to build strong and healthy bonds with others.

What you can do:

- Talk to your child about what a relationship is and how it works. Explain that relationships involve give and take and that everyone involved should be treated with respect.

- Help your child understand the importance of communication in a relationship. Teach them how to express their needs and feelings calmly and effectively.

- Encourage your child to resolve conflicts peacefully. Show them how to compromise and negotiate with others.

- Model respectful behavior yourself. Treat your child, partner, and others with kindness and courtesy.

By teaching your child about relationships, you can help them build strong and healthy bonds with others.

By being a good role model, you can set the foundation for your child to have positive and fulfilling relationships throughout their life.

Don't forget, you can always reach out to a parenting coach or counselor for support in teaching your child about relationships. They can offer additional tips and resources to help you and your family.

Unhealthy relationships can make young kids feel icky. Help them understand relationship basics so they can develop positive, healthy bonds with others.

Teach your child about relationships early on by modeling respectful behavior, talking about communication, and encouraging conflict resolution.

These skills will help them build strong, healthy bonds with others throughout their life.

If you need support, reach out to a parenting coach or counselor. They can offer additional tips and resources to help you and your family.

One of the most important things you can do as a parent is teaching your child about relationships. By understanding relationship dynamics, your child can develop healthier and more positive relationships with others.

As a parent, you are your child's first teacher when it comes to learning about relationships. You can set a good example by maintaining healthy and positive relationships with your own partner, family, and friends.

You can also talk to your child about relationship issues, such as communication, conflict resolution, and respect.

By teaching your child about relationships, you can help them develop the skills they need to build strong and healthy bonds with others.

CHAPTER FIVE

The Types of Relationship your Child Must KNOW

When parenting, it's important to help your child understand different types of relationships. This will enable them to develop healthy relationships themselves, and navigate complex social situations as they grow up.

There are four main types of relationships: familial, platonic, romantic, and professional.

Familial relationships are those between family members. These can be further divided into nuclear (immediate) families and extended ones (including cousins, aunts, uncles, etc).

Platonic relationships are non-romantic friendships. They may be between people of the same or different genders.

Romantic relationships are between two people who are attracted to each other and may have sexual feelings for each other.

Professional relationships are between people who work together. These can be formal or informal relationships.

It's important to teach your child about these different types of relationships so that they can identify them in their own lives and develop healthy relationships themselves.

Every child is different and will need different amounts of guidance when it comes to understanding relationships. Some children may be able to understand these concepts quickly, while others may need more time.

The important thing is to be patient and to provide your child with the resources they need to learn about relationships in a safe and supportive environment.

Here are resources you can provide your child with;

- Books: Look for children's books that deal with relationships. These can be helpful in sparking discussions about the different types of relationships and how to identify them.

- Games: There are many games available that focus on social skills and relationships. These can be a fun way for your child to learn about different types of relationships.

- Movies and TV shows: There are many movies and TV shows that deal with relationships. These can be a great way to start a discussion with your child about the different types of relationships.

- Online resources: There are many websites that provide information about relationships. These can be a great way to get more information or find resources that you can use with your child.

Here is how to begin a relationship talk with your child;

- Choose a time when you and your child are both relaxed and have some time to talk.

- Start by asking your child what they know about relationships. This will give you an idea of where to start the conversation.

- Use age-appropriate language to explain different types of relationships.

- Encourage your child to ask questions and express their thoughts and feelings about relationships.

- Provide resources that your child can use to learn more about relationships.

- Check-in with your child periodically to see how they are doing with understanding different types of relationships.

Scenarios are a great way to teach your child about different types of relationships. You can use the following scenarios to start a discussion with your child about relationships;

-Your child is playing with a friend and they get into a disagreement. What types of relationships are involved in this scenario?

-Your child is talking to their teacher about a project. What type of relationship is involved in this scenario?

-Your child is spending time with their grandparents. What type of relationships are involved in this scenario?

-Your child is going on a date with someone they met online. What type of relationship is involved in this scenario?

Take some time to talk with your child about these different types of relationships. This will help them to understand the different types of relationships and how to identify them.

It is also important to provide resources that your child can use to learn more about relationships.

These resources can be found online, in books, or through games and movies. Check in with your child periodically to see how they are doing with understanding different types of relationships.

Age Appropriate Relationships for Your Child

Parenting is not easy, but one of the most important things you can do is teach your child about healthy relationships. With a strong foundation, your child will be better equipped to navigate the complicated world of social interactions.

One way to help your child understand relationships is to introduce the concept of different types of relationships. Here are a few age-appropriate examples:

* For preschoolers: explain that some people are friends, some are family, and some are acquaintances.

Help them understand that each type of relationship has different expectations and boundaries.

Healthy and unhealthy relationships

As your child grows older, they will likely start to develop romantic interests. It's important to talk with them about both healthy and unhealthy relationships. Here are some things to keep in mind:

healthy relationships involve:

- communication

- respect

- trust

- support

- healthy conflict resolution

unhealthy relationships involve:

- put downs or criticism

- controlling behavior

- jealousy or possessiveness

- unrealistic expectations or demands

- Violence, either physical or emotional

If you're concerned that your child may be in an unhealthy relationship, talk with them about it. Help them to identify red flags and encourage them to come to you if they ever feel unsafe. As a parent, you can also model healthy relationships in your own life.

Here are a few age-appropriate relationship examples;

3-5 years old: healthy relationships involve sharing, taking turns, and using kind words. Unhealthy relationships involve hitting, biting, or pushing.

6-8 years old: healthy relationships involve cooperating, listening to each other, and being honest. Unhealthy relationships involve yelling, name-calling, or making threats.

9-12 years old: healthy relationships involve standing up for yourself and others, and being assertive but not aggressive.

Unhealthy relationships involve feeling scared or threatened by another person's words or actions.

It's never too early to start talking with your child about healthy relationships! By setting the foundation now, you can help them to develop healthy habits that will last a lifetime.

For example, you could:

- Read stories together that show healthy and unhealthy relationships.

- Talk about how characters in the story are treating each other.

- Help your child to identify their own feelings, and the feelings of others.

- Encourage your child to express themselves in healthy ways, such as through art, writing, or movement.

Beginning the Pornography TALK

There is no one answer to the question of how parents can educate their children about pornography. However, there are some general principles that can be followed.

First, it is important to remember that children are curious by nature and will likely seek out information about sex and sexuality on their own.

As a result, it is important for parents to provide accurate and age-appropriate information to their children.

This will help them to understand what they are seeing and make informed decisions about their own sexual behavior.

Second, parents should avoid shaming their children or making them feel guilty for being curious about sexuality.

Instead, they should create an open and honest dialogue where questions can be asked without judgment.

Lastly, there are a number of resources available to parents who want to educate their children about pornography.

These include books, websites, and even videos. By taking the time to educate themselves, parents can provide their children with the information they need to make responsible decisions about their own sexuality.

Instill sound values into your children from an early age. Help them understand that pornography is a form of exploitation and can be addictive.

Watch out for warning signs that they might be viewing pornography, such as secrecy, excessive use of the computer or phone, and changes in behavior.

If you suspect your child is viewing pornography, talk to them about it in a calm and non-judgmental way. Explain why you are concerned and offer support and resources to help them stop.

Pornography education should be an ongoing conversation within the family.

As children grow older and become more curious about sex and sexuality, parents can continue to provide them with accurate information and answer any questions they may have.

By doing so, parents can help their children develop healthy attitudes towards sex and sexuality.

Make sure you let your child knows the following effects of pornography and bad images online;

-It is addictive

-It warps views of relationships and sex

-Can desensitize someone to violence

-Can lead to acting out sexually

With this in mind, approach the conversation in a manner that is respectful, nonjudgmental, and factual. **Here are some tips:**

-Start early. It is important to have these conversations with your kids before they are exposed to pornography.

-Be proactive. Take the time to discuss what a healthy relationship looks like and what consent means.

-Set boundaries and expectations. Let your child know that you are available to talk about anything they see or hear that makes them feel uncomfortable.

-Monitor their internet usage. Use parental controls and monitoring tools to help you keep track of what your child is doing online.

-Teach them to be critical consumers of media. Help them understand that not everything they see online is true or accurate.

-Talk about respect for others. Emphasize that everyone deserves to be treated with respect, no matter how they look or what they do.

-Keep the lines of communication open. Make it clear to your child that they can talk to you about any worries or issues they may have.

There are several methods that parents can teach their kids about cyberbullying. One tactic is to define cyberbullying for children and highlight the reasons why it is inappropriate. Make sure your child is aware of the significant repercussions that cyberbullying may have on both the victim and the bully.

Additionally, you must convey to your kid the seriousness of cyberbullying and the need of not laughing it off.

Providing your child with examples of cyberbullying is another method to help them comprehend it.

Numerous websites and social media services allow users to publish cruel or offensive comments anonymously.

Showing your child examples of this type of behavior can help them understand how harmful it can be.

Last but not least, you should urge your kid to contact you if they ever encounter or see cyberbullying. Tell them you'll take it seriously and support them in resolving the issue.

Talking to your child about cyberbullying can be challenging, but it is crucial that they are aware of the dangers.

Understanding Cyber Bullying;

When someone intentionally hurts or is cruel to another person online, it is called cyberbullying. It can take many forms, including:

- Posting mean or hurtful comments about someone on social media

- Sending anonymous threatening or abusive messages

- Posting someone else's embarrassing images or videos without their consent- Pretending to be someone else online in order to trick someone into revealing personal information

- Both the victim and the bully may experience severe repercussions as a result of cyberbullying.

Victims may experience anxiety, depression, low self-esteem, and even thoughts of suicide.

Bullies may also suffer from social isolation and mental health problems.

Cyberbullying has occasionally had tragic outcomes, including school shootings. Make sure your kids understand the danger of cyberbullying by having a conversation with them about it.

If you believe that a crime has been committed and you think that your child may be a victim of cyberbullying, you should get in touch with local law enforcement.

How Can Parents Help?

To assist stop cyberbullying, parents can do the following:

- Explain the dangers of cyberbullying to your kids and make sure they understand what it is.

- Help your children comprehend the serious consequences that can result from cyberbullying.

- Give pupils concrete instances to illustrate the harm that online abuse may cause.

- Remind your kids to get in touch with you if they ever encounter or see cyberbullying.

- If your child complains of being bullied online, take the claim seriously and work with them to find a resolution.

- Keep an eye on your kids' online activity and keep track of the social media sites and websites they frequent.

- Instruct your kids not to participate in cyberbullying themselves and to always be polite and respectful online.

Cyberbullying is a significant issue that can have terrible repercussions. Parents are crucial in preventing it from occurring.

You can contribute to making the internet a safer place for everyone by having a conversation with your kids about cyberbullying and teaching them how to behave online.

Recent years have seen an upsurge in cyberbullying, in part because of the popularity of social media.

Make sure your kids understand the danger of cyberbullying by having a conversation with them about it as a parent.

There are several options available to assist if you suspect that your child is a victim of cyberbullying.

SCENARIOS ON ONLINE BULLYING

Cyberbullying can happen in a variety of ways. It might be done by email, text messaging, or social media.

Parents must educate their children about the dangers of cyberbullying and how to prevent it.

One way to do this is to use scenarios.

For example, you could ask your child what they would do if they received a mean message from someone online.

Would they respond?

Ignore it?

Tell a trusted adult?

Talking through several scenarios with your child will help them understand how to respond to cyberbullying if it ever happens to them.

Keep in mind that cyberbullying may be just as destructive as traditional bullying.

It's crucial to discuss it with your kids so they understand how to stay safe online.

You can use the following scenarios to protect your child against online bullying:

NOTE: the questions after each scenario are questions you should ask your child to get responses and deal with the situation then.

Scenario 1:

Your child is on social media when they receive a message from a user they don't know. The message is mean and makes your child feel upset.

What would you do in this situation?

Scenario 2:

Your child is cyber bullying someone else. They didn't mean to hurt the person, but they can see that the person is upset.

What would you do in this situation?

Scenario 3:

Your child witness cyber bullying taking place. Even though they don't know the victim of the bullying, they can still tell how hurt they are.

What would you do in this situation?

You can teach your child understand what to do if they ever find themselves in a position similar by going over these many cyberbullying scenarios with them.

CHAPTER SIX

Common Sex Related Questions Your Child May Ask and How to Answer Them

You can also contact your local law enforcement if you believe that a crime has been committed.

If you're a parent, you've probably been dreading "the talk" with your child. But birds and bees discussions don't have to be awkward! Here are some tips for how to answer sex questions from your kids.

First, consider your child's age and development stage. The birds and bees conversation will look different depending on whether your child is 5 or 15. Make sure that you're providing information that is appropriate for your child's age and maturity level.

Second, be ready to respond to any queries that are raised.

You don't have to have all the answers, but it can help to do some research ahead of time so that you're not caught off guard.

Third, be honest in your answers. Kids can sense when their parents are being dishonest, and this can damage the trust between you.

Fourth, be open to continuing the conversation. Birds and bees discussions don't have to happen all at once. If your child has more questions later on, be willing to talk about it again.

Finally, remember that you're the parent and you get to decide what information is shared and when.

If you're not comfortable answering a particular question, you don't have to.

Just let your child know that you're not ready to talk about it yet and assure them that they can come to you with any questions they have.

Birds and bees discussions can be daunting for parents, but they don't have to be!

Here are questions and how to answer them;

1. How did I get here?

This is a tough question for many parents but being honest is always the best policy. You can tell them that two people who love each other very much decided to have a baby and that you are that baby.

2. Where do babies come from?

Again, honesty is the best policy. You can tell them that when a man and woman love each other very much, they might decide to have a baby and that's how you got here.

3. What is sex?

This is a difficult question to answer because it will depend on the age of your child. If they are younger, you can simply tell them that sex is when two people who love each other very much share their bodies with one another in a special way.

If they are older, you can give them more details about what happens during sex.

4. Is sex bad?

No, sex is not bad. However, it's important to teach your children about safe sex and why it's important to wait until they are ready before having sex.

5. Who can I talk to if I have more questions?

You! Let them know that you are always available to answer any questions they have. If they are embarrassed, assure them that there is nothing to be embarrassed about and that you will always be there for them.

6. What is love?

Love is when you have strong, positive feelings toward someone. It can be platonic (friendship), familial (between parents and children, siblings, etc.), or romantic (between partners).

7. What are genitals?

Genitals are the reproductive organs that make it possible for humans to have sex and reproduce. Men have penis and testicles while women have vaginas and ovaries.

8. How do I know if I'm gay, lesbian, bisexual, or transgender?

This is something that you will likely figure out as you get older and develop more of an attraction to people of the same or opposite gender than you currently are. For now, just focus on enjoying your life and growing up!

9. What is puberty?

Your body transitions from that of a child to that of an adult during puberty. During puberty, you will develop secondary sex characteristics (such as breasts or facial hair) and be able to reproduce.

10. I'm scared/nervous about Puberty, what should I do?

That's totally normal! You can talk to me about any concerns you have and I can help guide you through this time. Remember, everyone goes through it so you're not alone!

Using Scenarios to Answer Sex Related Questions

One of the best ways to answer your children's sex-related questions is to use scenarios. By providing them with real-life examples, they can better understand the concepts involved.

For example, if you're explaining how babies are made, you could tell them about a couple who decided to have a baby. You could describe how the woman's body changes during pregnancy, and how the baby is born.

Children will be more likely to understand and remember the information if it's presented in a relatable way. Plus, using scenarios can help take the pressure off of you as a parent.

You don't have to worry about getting all the details perfect, because the focus is on the children understanding the general idea.

So go ahead and give it a try. Using scenarios is a great way to answer your children's questions in a way that they'll understand.

Who knows, you could even gain something from the experience yourself!

One of the best ways to answer your children's sex-related questions is to use scenarios.

By providing them with real-life examples, they can better understand the concepts involved.

For example, if you're explaining how babies are made, you could tell them about a couple who decided to have a baby.

You could describe how the woman's body changes during pregnancy, and how the baby is born.

Children will be more likely to understand and remember the information if it's presented in a relatable way.

-A couple who decides to have a baby.

-How the woman's body changes during pregnancy.

-How the baby is born. Children will be more likely to understand and remember the information if it's presented in a relatable way.

By providing children with relatable examples, they can better understand the concepts involved in sex and remember the information presented to them.

So next time your children have a question about sex, try using a scenario to help explain things more clearly.

Children will be more likely to understand and remember the information if it's presented in a relatable way. Plus, using scenarios can help take the pressure off of you as a parent. You don't have to worry about getting all the details perfect.

-A woman's body changes during pregnancy

-The baby is born

-How babies are made

Now, you can use the following relatable scenarios to answer your child's sex related questions;

1. A couple who decides to have a baby:

You can describe how the woman's body changes during pregnancy, and how the baby is born.

Children will be more likely to understand and remember the information if it's presented in a relatable way. Plus, using scenarios can help take the pressure off of you as a parent. You don't have to worry about getting all the details perfect.

2. How babies are made:

You could tell them about a couple who decided to have a baby. You could describe how the woman's body changes during pregnancy, and how the baby is born.

Children will be more likely to understand and remember the information if it's presented in a relatable way. Plus, using scenarios can help take the pressure off of you as a parent. You don't have to worry about getting all the details perfect.

So next time your children have a question about sex, try using a scenario to help explain things more clearly.

You can model the previous scenarios to come up with relatable answers/scenarios for your child.

CONCLUSION

Sex education is an important part of psychology, particularly when it comes to 8-12 year olds. At this age, children are learning about the world around them and developing their understanding of sex.

It's important for parents and guardians to provide accurate, up-to-date information on sex in a supportive manner.

Sex education can help children better understand their bodies, relationships, boundaries and consent. This knowledge will be useful as they enter puberty and adulthood.

They will be able to make informed decisions about their own sexual health and safety.

It is important for children to receive comprehensive sex education that covers topics such as puberty and reproduction, gender identity, sexual orientation, contraception and safe sex practices. This educational approach should focus on respect, communication and consent. This can help children develop positive attitudes about sex, understand the importance of healthy relationships, and build better self-esteem.

Sex education should be tailored to the specific needs of each child. For example, parents may choose to discuss different topics at different times depending on their child's level of understanding.

It is also important to be aware of cultural or religious beliefs and avoid language that might make children uncomfortable.

Overall, sex education for 8-12 year olds should focus on providing accurate information in a supportive environment.

This can help ensure that children have the knowledge they need to make informed decisions about their sexual health in the future.

Hopefully, you will find anything and everything you will need to educate your loved little one... even if you are a teacher and parent.

Printed in Great Britain
by Amazon

18902355R00047